HORSES

Written by Sheena Grant
Illustrated by Diana Morice

an imprint of
SCHOLASTIC
www.scholastic.com

Scholastic and Tangerine Press and associated logos are trademarks of Scholastic Inc.
Published by Tangerine Press, an imprint of Scholastic Inc., 557 Broadway, New York, NY 10012
10 9 8 7 6 5 4 3 2 1
0-439-78527-8
Printed and bound in China

Contents

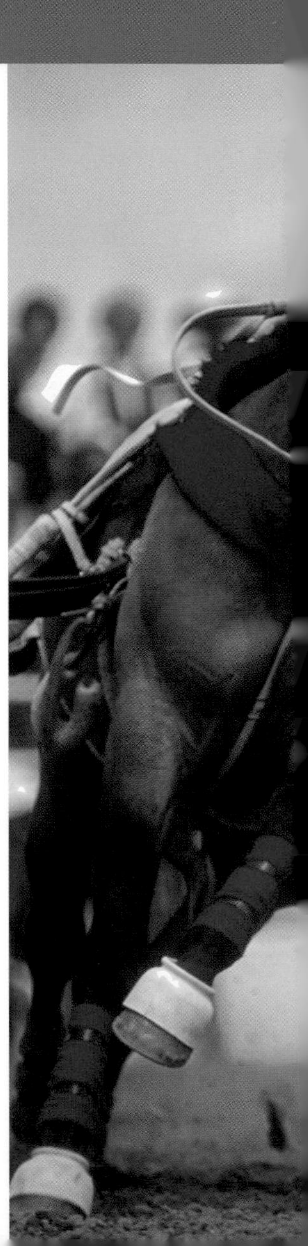

Horses and people share a history that dates back thousands of years. We credit horses for much of society's survival and progress, first for food and later in wars, on the roads, in farming, and in industry.

Equus

Horses belong to the Equus family. Equus comes from an ancient Greek word meaning "quickness." Horses are mammals in the same family as donkeys, zebras, and mules.

Did You Know?

Horses are measured in hands from the ground to the withers, or front shoulders. A hand is 4 in (10.1 cm). The letters "hh" stand for "hands high." You can tell a horse's approximate age by its teeth. A pony is a small horse (less than 14.2 hands). Of the 150 breeds of horses and ponies, the Thoroughbred is the fastest.

A New Role

As years passed, machinery took over the work that horses once performed. Nowadays we own and ride horses for pleasure.

History of Riding

One of the earliest records of man riding a horse is an engraving on bone that is about 5,000 years old. Horses were useful to human beings because of their speed, strength, bravery, and willingness to cooperate.

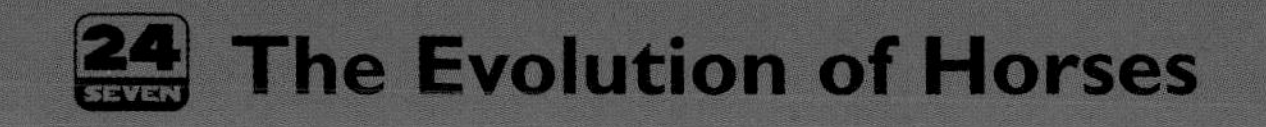

The Evolution of Horses

The Beginning

Modern horses descended from the Eohippus, an animal that lived more than 50 million years ago in what is now North America. The map of the world was very different then. Horses were able to move across land from North America to Asia, Africa, and Europe. Since then, rising sea levels have closed these land routes and sea now separates the continents. For some unknown reason, horses became extinct in America. They were reintroduced by European colonists thousands of years later.

Eohippus

About the size of a fox, Eohippus had four toes, short hair, a thick neck and a stumpy tail. It ate by picking at shrubs rather than grazing.

Early cave paintings show that horses existed thousands of years ago.

Evolution

As the weather and plant life changed on Earth, Eohippus had to change as well to survive. Over millions of years it evolved, in stages, into an animal with longer legs, able to run faster to escape from animals that might harm it. As a result, it gradually lost its four toes. Modern horses now stand on a single hoof. Its neck is longer for grazing on grasses and ground plants.

Still Wild at Heart

Despite all the years living with man, horses still have the skills to survive in the wild. They are herd animals and enjoy the company of other horses. They are happiest when grazing with their friends, rather than being left alone in stables for many hours at a time. When they are frightened, their instinct is to run away, as they would have done in the wild many thousands of years ago.

Horses grazing in a field.

Equus Caballus

Eventually, the modern horse, Equus Caballus, emerged. Nearly 6,000 years ago, man domesticated, or tamed, the horse.

Parts of a Horse

Poll: *The bony area between the ears. Except for the ears, it is the highest point on the horse's body when it is standing with its head up.*

Forehead: *Should be broad, full, and flat.*

Nostrils: *Should be able to open wide to take in maximum air for breathing.*

Muzzle: *The end of a horse's nose that is velvety to touch.*

Point of Shoulder: *A hard, bony surface that stands out, surrounded by big muscle areas.*

Elbow: *The bony area lying against the chest at the beginning of the forearm.*

Knee: *The joint below the forearm.*

Fetlock: *The joint below the cannon bone.*

Pastern: *Runs from the fetlock to the top of the hoof.*

Shoulder: *Should be covered with flat muscle and blend well into the withers.*

Neck: *Lightweight horses should have reasonably long necks for good appearance and proper balance.*

Chest: *A good chest is deep and contains enough space for vital organs. Depth is the distance from the withers to the elbow.*

Breast: *A muscle area between the forelegs, covering the front of the chest.*

Forearm: *The area of foreleg from the elbow to the knee. The forearm should be muscular.*

Cannon: *The long bone below the knee. Visible from the front of the leg, it should be straight.*

Hoof: *The horny wall and the sole of the foot.*

Crest: *The curved top line of the neck. Not very noticeable in mares and usually fuller in stallions.*

Withers: *The bony ridge where the neck and the back join. The horses height is measured from the ground to the withers.*

Back: *Runs from the base of the withers to the last rib.*

Loins: *The short area joining the back to the powerful muscular croup (rump).*

Croup: *Located between the loins and the tail. Viewed from the side or back, it is the highest point of the hindquarters.*

Dock: *Flesh and bone section of a horse's tail from which the hair grows.*

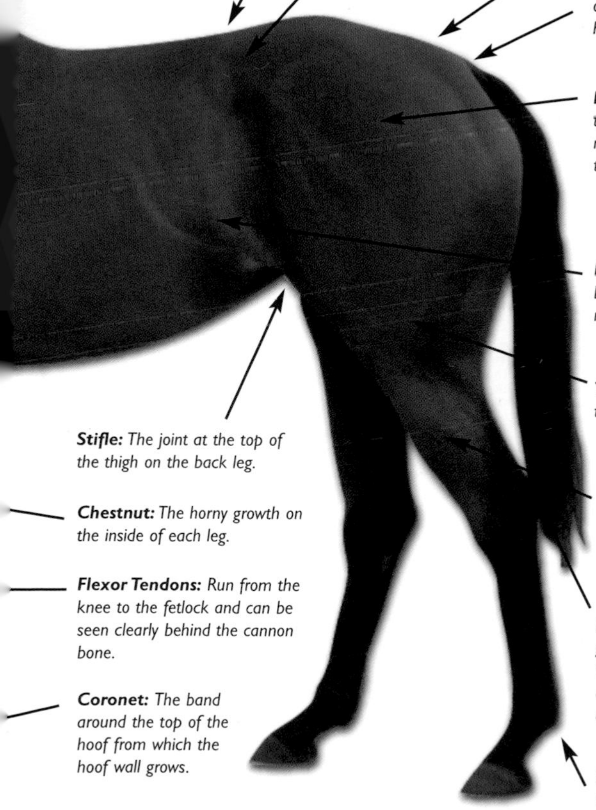

Hindquarters: *Gives power to the horse. Should be muscular when viewed from the side and back.*

Flank: *The area below the loins between the last rib and the massive thigh muscles.*

Thigh: *Muscled area at the top of the back leg.*

Stifle: *The joint at the top of the thigh on the back leg.*

Gaskin: *The region, sometimes called the second thigh, between the stifle and the hock.*

Chestnut: *The horny growth on the inside of each leg.*

Flexor Tendons: *Run from the knee to the fetlock and can be seen clearly behind the cannon bone.*

Hock: *The joint between the gaskin and the cannon bone. The bony piece that sticks out at the back of the hock is called the point of hock.*

Coronet: *The band around the top of the hoof from which the hoof wall grows.*

Heel: *Area above the back of the hoof.*

Horse Gaits

Horses have four natural gaits, or ways of moving. At a gallop, they are among the fastest animals on Earth.

The Walk

A four-beat gait in which the horse moves one leg after another so that four hoof beats can be heard.

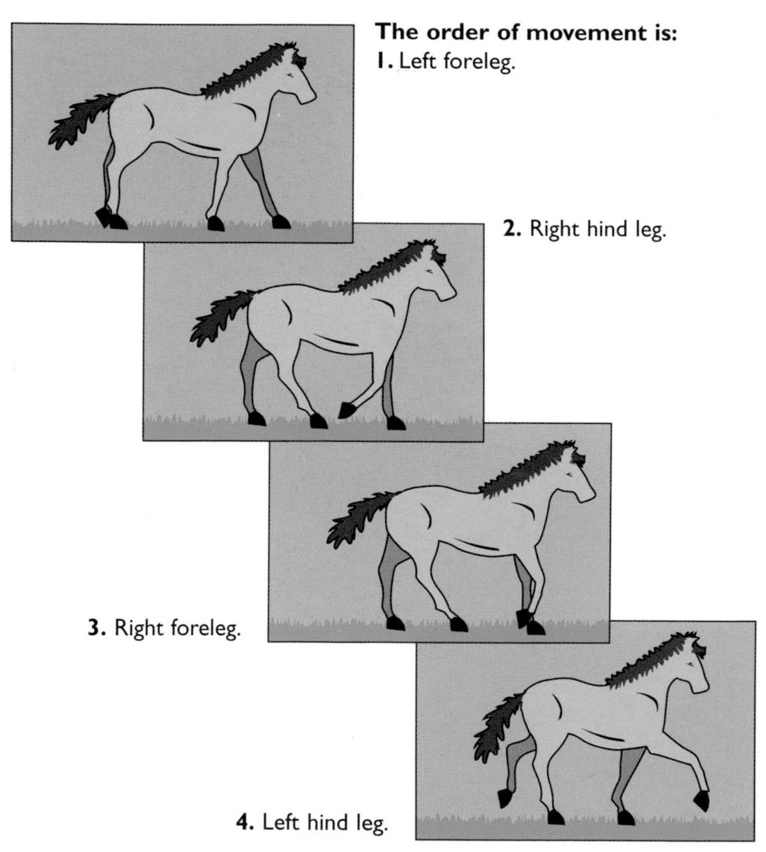

The order of movement is:

1. Left foreleg.

2. Right hind leg.

3. Right foreleg.

4. Left hind leg.

The Trot

A two-beat gait in which the horse moves opposite, or diagonal, hind and forelegs together.

The order of movement is:

1. Left foreleg and right hind leg leave the ground.

2. The horse then springs to the opposite of right foreleg and left hind leg. This happens before the left foreleg and right hind leg return to the ground. There is, therefore, a brief moment when all four legs are off the ground together.

When this happens, the rider finds it difficult to sit in the saddle. To overcome this, the rider rises out of the saddle and sits again when the horse's legs return to the ground (rising trot).

Horse Gaits

The Canter

A three-beat gait in which the horse moves in bounds, with either the right or left foreleg leading. If the horse is cantering on a circle to the right, it should lead with its right foreleg. On a circle to the left, it leads with its left foreleg.

Cantering to the right, the order of movement is:

1. Left hind leg.

2. Right hind leg and left foreleg move forward together.

3. Right foreleg.

4. All four legs are off the ground together – a moment of suspension.

The Gallop

This is a four-beat gait.

The sequence is usually as follows:

1. Left hind leg.

2. Right hind leg.

3. Left foreleg.

4. Right foreleg, followed by a moment of suspension when all four legs are off the ground at the same time.

Coat Colors and Markings

The colors and markings of horses have fascinated people for generations. As you'll see, every horse has its own unique coloring. To identify a horse, take a look at their points (muzzle, tips of ears, tail, and lower legs).

Dun

Color ranges from sandy/yellow to reddish/brown, with the legs often darker than the bodies. Some have "zebra" stripes on the legs. All have a "dorsal" stripe along the middle of the back.

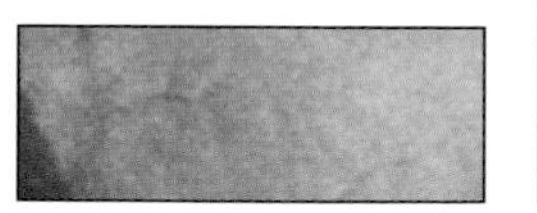

Roan

A "Blue Roan" is a black or brown horse with a sprinkling of white. A "Strawberry Roan" is a chestnut horse with a sprinkling of white, as pictured.

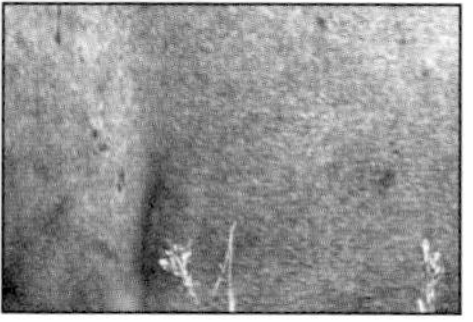

Chestnut

Ginger, yellow or reddish color with mane and tail of a similar color, or flaxen. The three shades of chestnut are dark, liver and light.

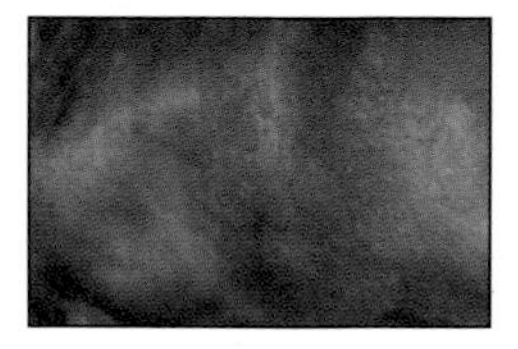

Gray

Mix of white and black hairs, growing paler with age, on black skin. Can be dappled, as pictured.

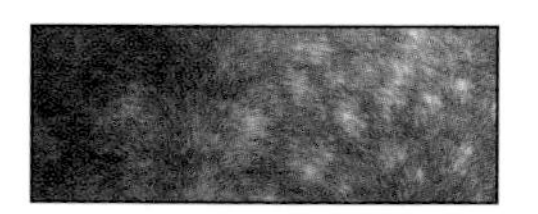

Creamello

Cream-colored coat on pinkish skin. Although the eyes are blue, they often look pinkish.

Black

Coat, legs, mane, and tail are black. Markings can be white.

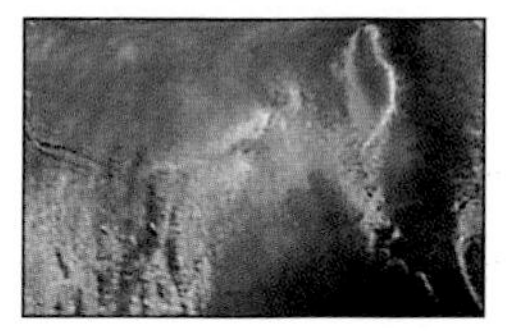

Palomino

Golden color with white or flaxen mane and tail.

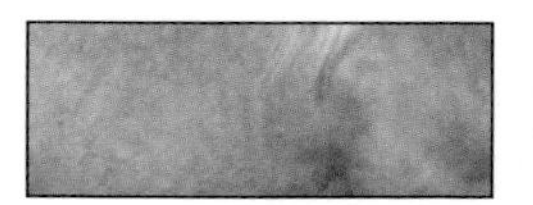

Bay

Any brownish color with black mane, tail, and points.

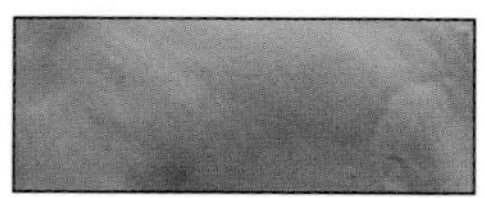

Pinto

Marked with patches of white.

Markings

These show areas of white on the head, body, and legs.

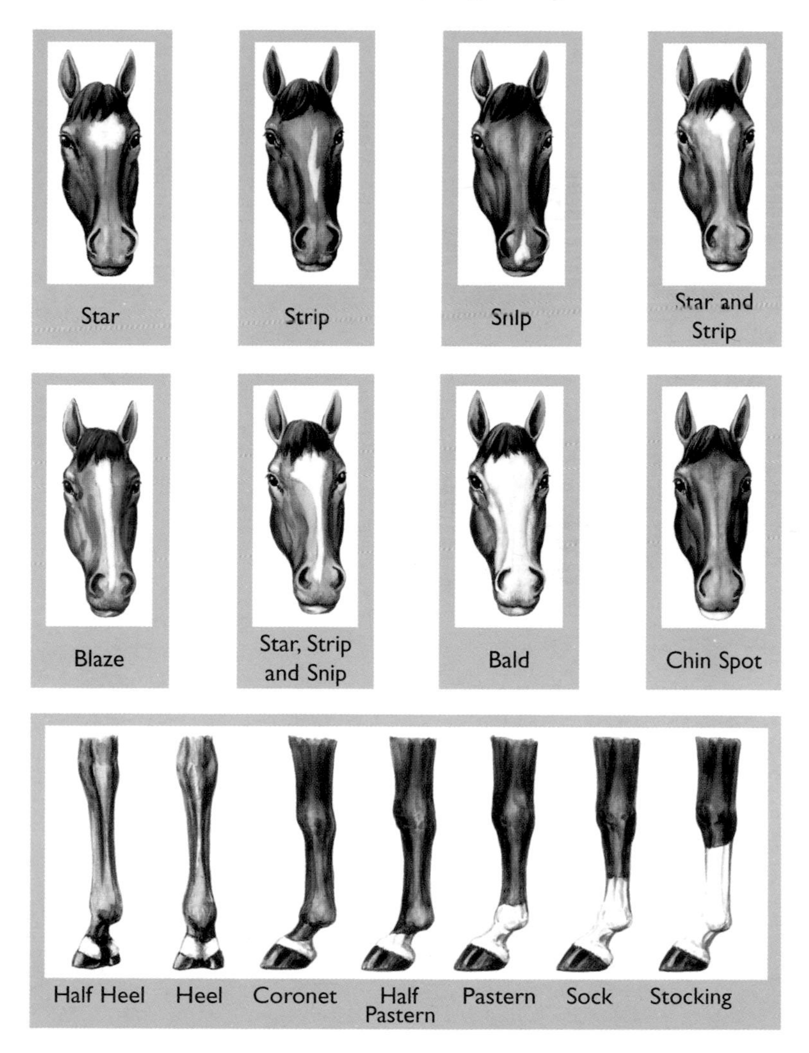

Horse Types

There are many different types of horses suitable for different jobs and different people. A type of horse is not necessarily a specific breed – it can be a mixture of more than one.

Cob

A strong and stocky animal with short, powerful legs. He should be large in the body and have a head showing as much quality, or fineness, as possible. The cob should be no bigger than 15.3hh, and should have a good temperament.

Cobs are often used as cart horses.

Hunter

The type of horse used for hunting depends on the kind of countryside where it will be riding. Generally, the hunter should have a strong cannon bone, enabling it to carry weight. Usually half or three-quarters Thoroughbred, it should also have strong hindquarters to give a powerful jump and be able to carry riders safely and comfortably. In British show classes, hunters are often divided into heavyweight, middleweight, and lightweight groups, depending on the amount of weight they are capable of carrying.

Hunter horses are very well trained and kept in good condition.

National Show Horse

A horse popular in America. It ideally has a blend of the Arab horse's beauty, refinement, strength, and stamina with the American Saddlebred's extremely long neck, high-stepping action, and show-ring style.

Show horses need to be very patient, as performing can be very tiring.

Polo Pony

These are fast, athletic Thoroughbreds. They are always called ponies, whatever their height. They are wiry and tough and are able to carry a large man at a gallop. They need to be able to turn, stop, and speed up quickly and brave enough to cope with the rough and tumble of the sport.

Polo ponies have to be brave as polo can be a challenging sport.

Hack

Usually pure or mostly Thoroughbred, the hack is a quality lightweight riding horse suitable for general riding. A top-quality hack will have excellent movement and self-balance. Years ago, hacks were the leisure horses ridden by wealthy citizens, so they had to look good and have excellent manners.

Canadian Mounties use horses as their mode of transport.

Horse Care Basics

Many horses are kept outside in the field, especially in the summer. However, most are stabled part of the time, generally at night during winter.

Reasons for Stabling

Stabling makes it easier to ensure a horse is safe and warm and has enough food to work. Stabling also makes it easier to keep them clean and ready to be ridden. Some breeds of horse, such as Thoroughbreds, need the protection of a stable from the weather.

Stable Routine

Dirty bedding and droppings should be removed each day. This is called mucking out. Horses are often given a morning feed before being sent to a field for the day or ridden. (You should always wait for at least an hour after feeding before riding, to allow the horse to digest its food.) They are then brought in at night, given hay and an evening feed. Water should be available at all times.

Stable Requirements

The stable should be big enough for a horse to move around and lie down comfortably. A good size for a pony would be 10 ft x 12 ft (3 m x 3.5 m) and, for a bigger horse, 12 ft x 14 ft (3.5 m x 4.2 m). The door should be 4 ft (1.2 m) wide and 8 ft (2.4 m) high and should be divided into upper and lower sections.

A horse's stable is important, especially in winter, to keep it warm, dry, and comfortable.

Bedding

Bedding makes the stable warm, comfortable, and safe. The most commonly used types are straw, wood shavings, and shredded paper.

There are several types of food for a horse, depending on how much energy it needs for the amount of exercise it is doing. Many horses live on grass during the summer. But if they are working hard, they need extra food for energy. All horses need extra food during the winter. They should eat about 2.5% of their bodyweight daily. Most should be roughage, such as hay.

Hay

Cut and dried grass. The main diet of most horses, especially in winter.

Concentrate Foods

Examples of concentrate foods are bran produced from milled wheat, high-energy grains such as oats, and barley, and maize, and chaff, a mix of hay and straw. Another example is sugar beet, which must be soaked before feeding.

Succulent Foods

Succulent foods are items such as carrots and apples.

Compound Foods

Compound foods, such as nuts, cubes, or coarse mixes, are ready-mixed alternatives to concentrates and are available for horses with a number of different energy needs.

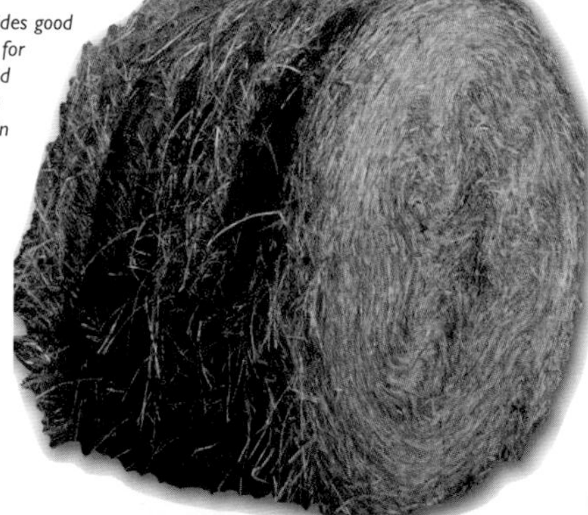

Hay provides good roughage for horses and should be included in their diet.

24 SEVEN Tools for Grooming

Looking after a horse is a big responsibility that takes a lot of time, knowledge, and money. Stabled horses need grooming every day; grass-kept horses less so, as they need oils in their coat for protection from the weather. Hooves also need regular attention.

Body Brush
Removes dust and grease from the coat, mane, and tail after using the dandy brush.

Dandy Brush
Removes heavier mud, especially from grass-kept horses. May be too harsh for sensitive-skinned horses.

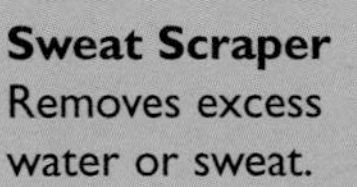

Sweat Scraper
Removes excess water or sweat.

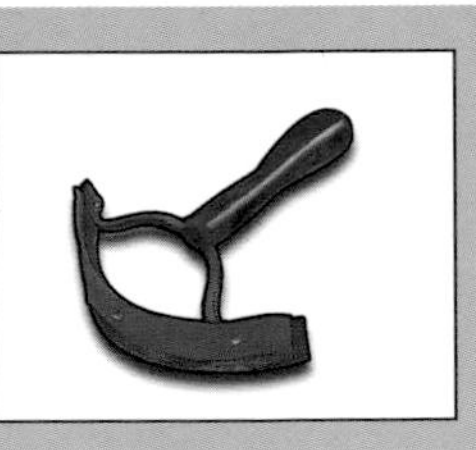

Hoof Pick
Removes mud and stones from the feet. Used from the horse's heel toward the toe.

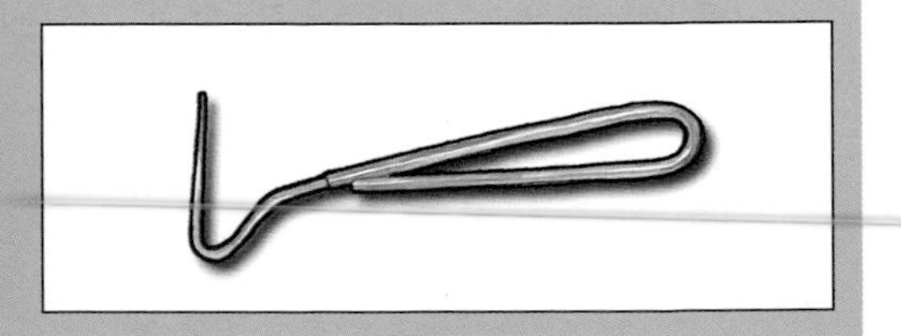

Tools for Grooming

Sponges
Separate ones for the eyes, nostrils, and dock.

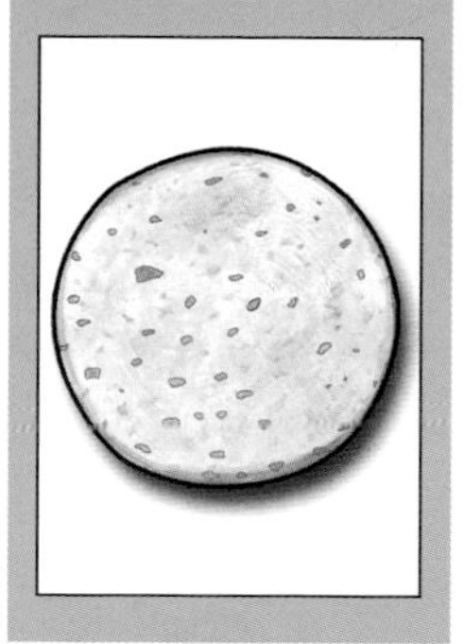

Stable Rubber
Linen cloth that gives a final polish after grooming.

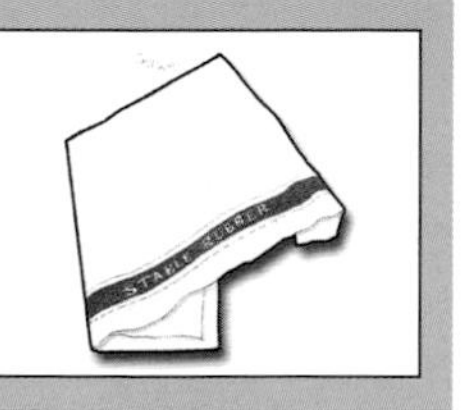

Metal Curry Comb
Used for cleaning the body brush.

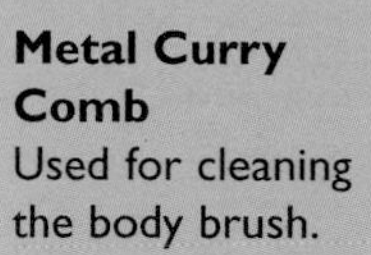

Rubber or plastic Curry Comb
Used in a circular motion for removing loose hair from a moulting or mud-covered horse.

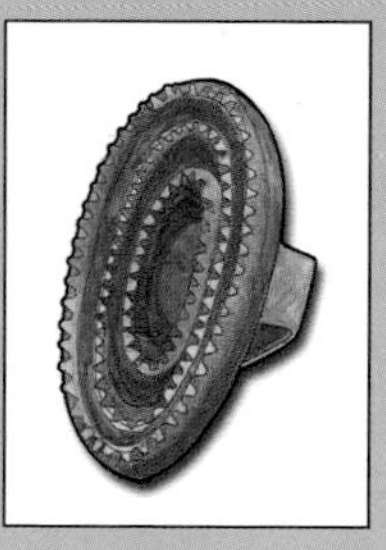

Water Brush
Use dampened on the mane, tail, and feet.

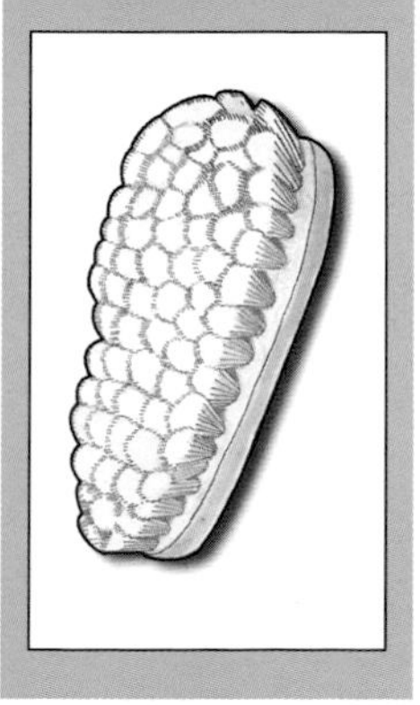

Mane and Tail Comb
For untangling and pulling (shortening and thinning) manes and tails.

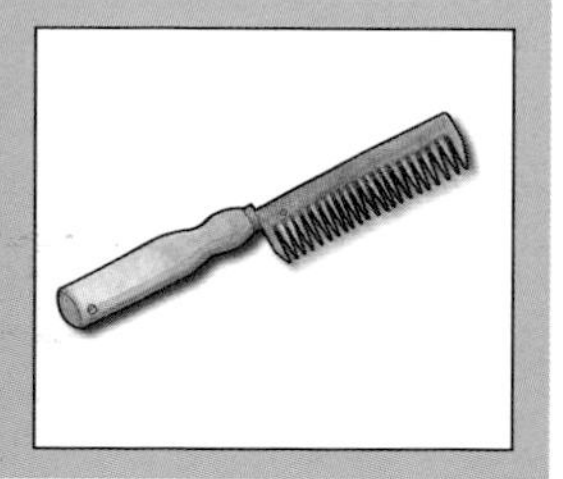

Clean and Healthy

Quartering is the quick removal of stable stains and obvious dirt before exercising. The feet should also be cleaned and the eyes, nostrils, and dock sponged.

Strapping is the main grooming session, often done after exercise when the horse is warm.

Lay (smooth) the mane with a dampened water brush.

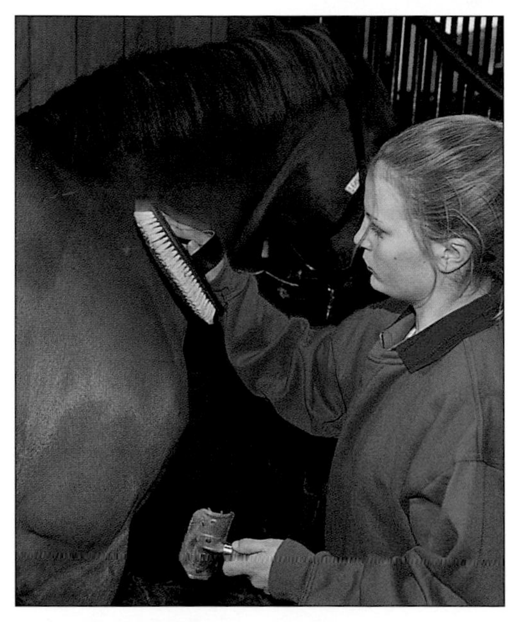

It is very important to keep your horse well-groomed.

Sponge out the eyes, nostrils and, using a separate sponge, the dock.

Starting at the top of the neck, move the body brush in short, circular strokes in the direction the coat grows. Use firm strokes, and clean the body brush with the metal curry comb after every few strokes. Gently groom the head with the body brush. Beginning groomers should be assisted by an experienced adult.

Clean and Healthy

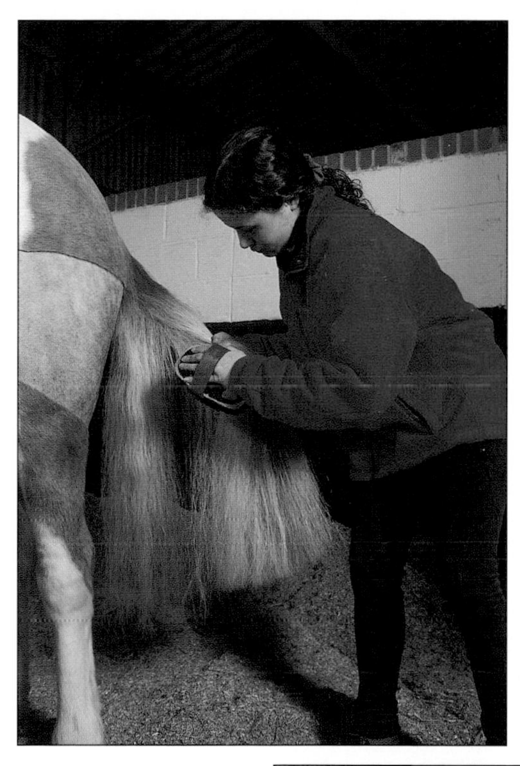

Use the body brush to untangle and brush out the mane and tail. Don't use the dandy brush or metal curry comb. This could hurt the horse and break the mane and tail hair.

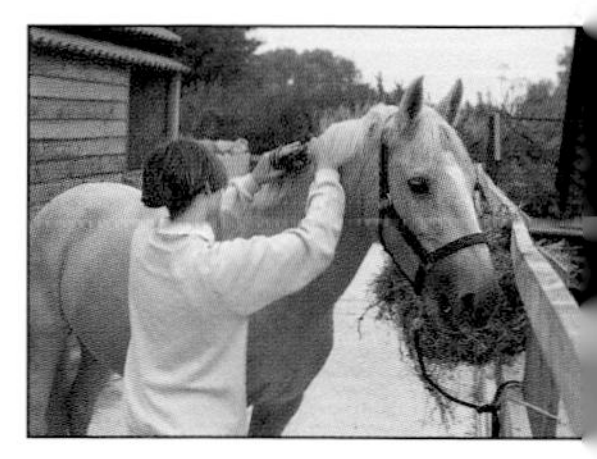

Use a dandy brush to remove mud or sweat marks (not on clipped or thin-skinned horses).

Hoof care is vital to ensure your horse does not go lame.

Use a body brush to gently untangle the horse's man – take care not to hurt it.

Oil the hooves, pick out the feet and check the shoes.

Use a damp stable rubber to give a final polish.

Grooming Tips

In the summer, horses may need to be washed if they return to the stable sweaty after exercise. A bucket of slightly warm water should be used to sponge the horse, just on the sweaty areas or all over. The horse should not be bathed every day because it would remove too many natural oils from its coat.

Other Grooming Tips:

1. Always tie the horse up when grooming.
2. Check the horse over for injuries, cuts or bruises.
3. If using a tail bandage to get the tail to lie flat after grooming or washing, don't leave it on for more than half an hour, as it could interfere with circulation.
4. Use this time to aquaint the horse to being handled and to build up your relationship with your equine friend.
5. Remember why you groom a horse – for cleanliness, condition, appearance, and for good health and circulation.

After washing, the sweat scraper should be used to remove excess water from the coat. A cooler or sweat rug should then be put on to keep the horse warm while he is drying.

If the horse is wet from being sponged, it is a good idea to use a sweat rug to keep it worm.

Horseshoes

There is an old saying "no foot, no horse." It means that if a horse is lame or has bad feet it cannot be ridden. It's as true today as it was years ago. That is why hoof care is so important.

Lucky Horseshoe?

It is believed that horseshoes bring good luck. For this reason, sometimes they are given to brides on the wedding day.

Trimming and Shoeing

A farrier or blacksmith should care for a horse's feet roughly every four to six weeks. Their hooves need to be trimmed, whether or not they wear shoes. Celtic horsemen first used iron shoes on their mounts almost 2,000 years ago. Today, horse shoes have been improved, but they haven't changed much.

Why Use Shoes?

To protect the feet against wear and tear, provide grip, and correct hoof problems and conformation (physical) faults.

The Hoof

The horse's foot is divided into two parts: the outer, insensitive parts and the inner, sensitive parts. Insensitive parts include the outer wall, which is made of dense horn and is constantly growing, the sole, and the frog, a triangular shaped structure in the center of the foot. Sensitive parts include bones and cartilages.

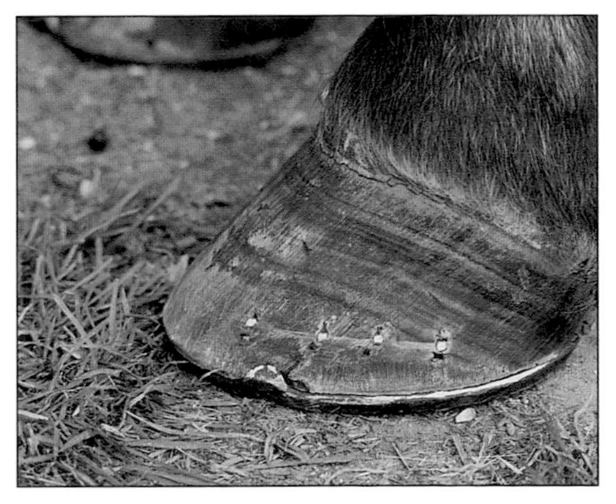

Horses hooves can be protected by the use of horseshoes.

Horse Shoes

Shoeing Tools

A farrier uses a number of tools. These include: a hammer; buffer to cut off clenches (flattened nail ends); pinchers to lift the clenches and lever off the shoes; hoof cutters; drawing knife and toeing knife for trimming the feet; rasp to level the surface of the feet; and a tripod to support the hoof while finishing off.

Daily Hoofcare

Hoof care isn't just the job of the farrier. Owners need to make sure they pick out the horse's hooves daily, keep the stable bed clean, check the wear of shoes, remove and replace shoes when necessary, and use a hoof treatment for protection.

Your horse's hooves should be checked daily.

Shoeing Procedure

The old shoes are removed and the hoof trimmed. The horse cannot feel this as the hoof wall is insensitive. The farrier may hot or cold shoe the horse. Hot shoeing involves heating the shoe in a forge, hammering it into shape, and placing it on the hoof, where it burns a brown rim, to see if it is a good fit. The horse does not feel this. In cold shoeing, the shoes are not heated before fitting, so the fit is not as good.

A farrier, or blacksmith, will shape a horse's shoe upon an anvil.

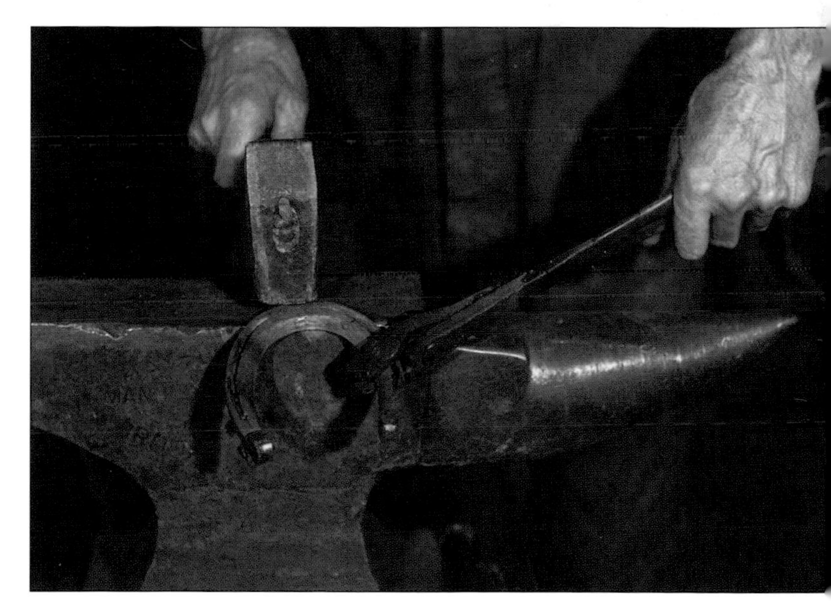

Shoe Nails

Seven nails secure the shoe on each hoof and are hammered into the insensitive part of the foot. The farrier must be careful to avoid the sensitive, inner parts of the foot. The nails are made so that they bend away from these as they are being hammered in. The hoof is finished off by cutting a bed for the shoe's toe clip. The trimmed nail endings, or clenches, are hammered flat, and the join between the hoof and shoe is filed smooth.

24 SEVEN Horse Riding

Horse riding is a popular sport. While it is great fun to both ride and care for horses, it is important to remember it is a risky sport. For this reason, lessons at a good riding school are vital for anyone wishing to learn how to ride and look after horses properly.

Where to Learn

Choose an approved riding school where you will be paired with a horse suited to your ability and where you can learn not just how to control the horse, but how to sit properly and develop a secure position. You will also be taught how to handle horses and how to ride correctly over jumps, as well as other skills as your riding improves.

It is important to ride safely – learn to ride at an approved riding school.

Riding Basics

The rider controls the horse through the use of "aids," which are the methods used to communicate with the horse. To communicate properly with the horse, the rider must be able to sit still and quietly in the saddle and apply the aids lightly and in a coordinated way. Otherwise, the horse may become confused and not understand what the rider is asking.

Any competition involving horses requires a lot of skill.

Horse riders can progress to competion level once they have gained a high level of experience and training.

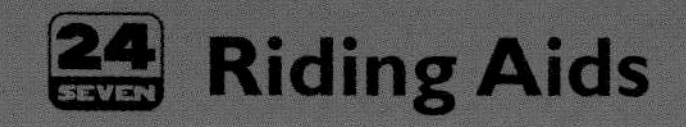

Riding Aids

Hand Aids

These are used to control and direct the energy created by asking the horse to move forward with the legs. The rider's contact with the horse's mouth through the reins should be light and flexible and follow the natural movement of the horse's head and neck. The hand aids are used with the leg aids and the seat aids to ask the horse to slow down, speed up, stop, or change direction. If a rider is too heavy with his or her hands, the horse may pull against the rider to try to escape the discomfort. A good rider will always have light hands.

International competition riders have many years' experience in the saddle.

Leg Aids

The horse is a flight animal, which means it reacts to danger by running away. So, when pressure from the rider's legs is applied, the horse moves forward to escape. This pressure should be quick series of vibrations with the inside leg or calf and never a heavy thump. More experienced riders can use leg aids in a variety of other ways; for example, to get the horse to move sideways and indicate which leg to lead on in canter.

Seat Aids

A flexible, relaxed, and secure seat allows the rider to absorb the horse's movement, letting the horse move freely and lightly and allowing horse and rider to move as one. The rider must develop a good seat to communicate effectively with the horse. The hand and leg aids can then be applied almost invisibly. Hands, legs, and seat are natural aids, along with the use of voice and body weight. Artificial aids are the whip and spurs. They should only be used to back up natural aids.

A good saddle is vital for the comfort of both the rider and horse.

Clothing for Riding

Riding Boots

Riding boots with a low heel are important. The heel stops your foot from slipping through the stirrup, which could be dangerous. Wellington boots are not suitable for riding.

The correct dress is important for keeping the rider safe.

A Riding Hat

This is essential for protection and should feature the latest safety standards.

Jodhpurs

These protect the legs from rubbing and do not ride up, which would be uncomfortable and make the rider unstable.

Tack

The major items include: saddle, girth, stirrup irons and leathers, bridle, throatlatch, browband, and noseband.

The **girth** goes around the horse's belly and holds the saddle in place. **Stirrup irons** are for your feet and **stirrup leathers** attach the stirrup irons to the saddle. The **bridle** is made up of a headpiece and cheekpieces, to which the bit is attached. The **throatlatch** and **browband** hold the headpiece in place. The bit goes into the horse's mouth, and reins are attached to the bit at one end and held by the rider at the other.

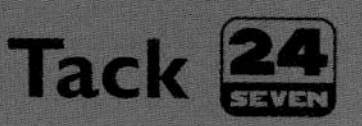

Horse racing requires different types of tack than those used in other forms of horse riding.

Tacking Up

Getting the horse ready for exercise by putting on the saddle and bridle is called tacking up. Saddles, bridles, stirrup leathers, and reins are usually made from leather, which needs to be cleaned regularly with saddle soap to keep it in good condition. Dirty tack would also irritate a horse's skin. The bit and stirrup irons are normally made from metal. There are many different types of bit for different horses and levels of control. Riding schools provide the tack you need to ride a horse. It is only if you buy a horse that you need to think about buying your own.

Guide to Light Horses

Akhal-Teke
Origins: Turkmenistan, to the north of Iran
Description: Wiry, bred to cope with extreme desert weather
Uses: Racing, competitions, endurance riding, and general riding
Height: 15.1hh to 15.2hh
Color: Bay, chestnut, gray, black

Andalucian
Origins: Spain
Description: Intelligent with an attractive movement, gentle nature, and strong, muscular body
Uses: All-around riding horse
Height: 15hh to 15.2hh
Color: Mainly grey and bay

Appaloosa
Origins: United States
Description: Compact, powerful-looking horse
Uses: Western, endurance riding, show ring
Height: 14.2hh to 15.2hh
Color: Distinctive white coat with black or brown spots, sparse mane and tail

Arab
Origins: The world's oldest pure breed which has a great influence on other breeds
Description: Light, graceful way of moving, is fast with great stamina. Distinctive dish face
Uses: General riding and racing as well as endurance
Height: 14.2hh to 15hh
Color: Usually bay or chestnut, but gray is common

Azteca
Origins: Mexico
Description: Versatile, good tempered, intelligent, agile, and elegant
Uses: General riding and competition
Height: 15.2hh to 16hh
Color: Any solid color

Criollo
Origins: Argentina
Description: Short, stocky head, and great stamina
Uses: Long distance and general riding
Height: 14hh to 15hh
Color: Usually dun with dark points

Canadian Horse
Origins: Canada, from French stock
Description: Well proportioned, solidly built
Uses: Varied
Height: 14hh to 16hh
Color: Black, but can range from bay to light chestnut

Colorado Ranger
Origins: United States
Description: Compact, refined horses with powerful hindquarters
Uses: Good working horses
Height: 15.2hh
Color: Any

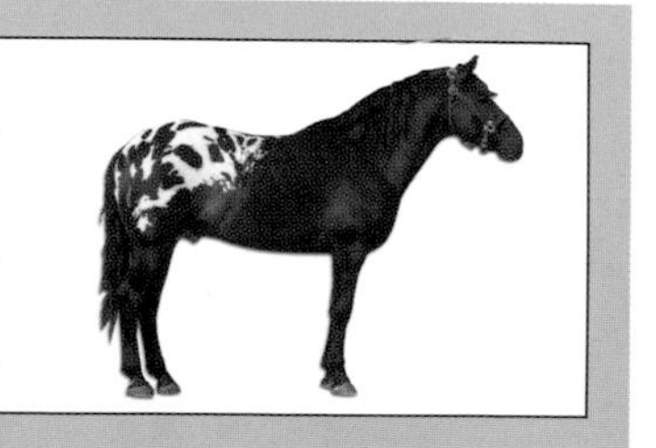

Florida Cracker
Origins: United States
Description: Small saddle horses with unusual ground covering gaits
Uses: Historically an important part of Florida's cattle industry
Height: 13hh to 15.2hh
Color: Any

Gelderlander
Origins: Netherlands
Description: Strong and active
Uses: General riding, driving, and competitions
Height: 16hh
Color: Chestnut, bay, or gray

Galiceno
Origins: Spain and Portugal
Description: Even-tempered, small, tough. Despite its size, the Galiceno is a horse with similar traits to others from the same geographical area. Has a distinctive running walk
Uses: General riding, competition
Height: 12hh to 13.2hh
Color: Any solid color

Dutch Groningen
Origins: Netherlands
Description: A steady, saddle horse
Uses: Riding and driving
Height: 15.3hh to 16.1hh
Color: Black, bay, or brown.

Hanoverian
Origins: Germany
Description: Honest temperament, strong, and athletic. Popular sports horse
Uses: Riding and driving, dressage, show-jumping
Height: 15.3hh to 16.2hh
Color: All solid colors

Holstein
Origins: Germany
Description: Strong, intelligent, and bold
Uses: General riding and competitions
Height: 16hh to 17hh
Color: Any

Irish Draught
Origins: Ireland
Description: Intelligent and kind temperament, natural balance
Uses: General riding, jumping
Height: Mares 15.2hh; stallions16.2hh
Color: Any solid color

Lipizzaner
Origins: Austria
Description: Intelligent and athletic. Famously used by the Spanish Riding School
Uses: Classical riding, dressage
Height: 15.1hh
Color: Gray or bay

Maremmana
Origins: Italy
Description: Solid and steady, cheap to feed
Uses: Many from agriculture to police and army horses
Height: 15.3hh
Color: Any solid color

Missouri Foxtrotter
Origins: United States
Description: "Fox trot" gait in which the horse walks with its forelegs and trots behind. Hind feet are slid rather than lifted to give a smooth ride
Uses: All modern leisure riding
Height: 14hh to 16hh
Color: Any

Morab
Origins: United States, bred from Morgans and Arabs
Description: Powerful horse with grace and refinement
Uses: Riding, driving, competition, endurance
Height: 14.2hh to 15.2hh
Color: Any

Morgan
Origins: United States
Description: Expressive head with large eyes
Uses: Riding and harness work
Height: 14.1hh to 15.2hh
Color: Bay, chestnut, black, or brown

Oldenburg
Origins: Germany
Description: The heaviest of German riding horses
Uses: Riding, driving
Height: 16hh to 17hh
Color: Black, brown, bay

Paso Fino
Origins: Latin America
Description: A light horse of great grace and style. Noted for its unusual gait. Paso means step and Fino means fine
Uses: Riding, show, cattle work
Height: Up to 15.2hh
Color: Any, except spotted

Quarter Horse
Origins: United States. Bred as quarter-mile sprinters
Description: Stocky with powerful hindquarters
Uses: Ranch horse, racing, rodeo work, polo, and general riding
Height: 14.3hh to 16hh
Color: Any solid color

Rocky Mountain
Origins: United States
Description: Gentle temperament with an easy four beat gait
Uses: General riding, endurance, competition
Height: 14.2hh to 16hh
Color: Any solid color

Guide to Light Horses

Saddlebred
Origins: United States
Description: Good looking and comfortable ride, high-stepping action
Uses: Riding or driving
Height: Average 15.3hh
Color: Usually chestnut, bay, brown, black, or gray. May be spotted, palomino or roan

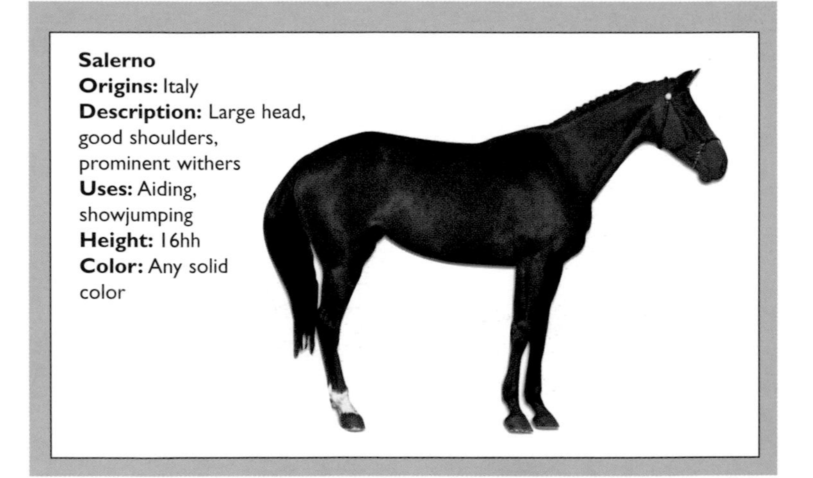

Salerno
Origins: Italy
Description: Large head, good shoulders, prominent withers
Uses: Aiding, showjumping
Height: 16hh
Color: Any solid color

Sardinian
Origins: Italy
Description: Tough with great stamina
Uses: Riding, competition, police work
Height: 15hh to 15.2hh
Color: Brown, bay

Selle Francais
Origins: France
Description: Athletic, looks similar to a Thoroughbred. Good competition horse
Uses: Jumping, competition
Height: 16hh
Color: Mainly chestnut

Standardbred
Origins: United States
Description: A tough breed that can trot nearly as fast as a Thoroughbred can gallop. Strong hindquarters and long back
Uses: Harness racing
Height: 14hh to 16hh
Color: Any solid color

Tennessee Walking Horse
Origins: United States
Description: Comfortable ride with high-stepping gaits and a fast, running walk
Uses: General riding, show
Height: 15.2hh
Color: Any

Thoroughbred
Origins: Developed in England in the 17th and 18th centuries from imported Oriental horses. Now the most valuable breed in the world
Description: Very fast and athletic
Uses: Excels in racing and competition riding. Has played a role in upgrading other breeds
Height: Variable, average 16hh
Color: Any solid color, gray, and roan

Trakehner
Origins: Germany.
Description: Similar in appearance to the Thoroughbred
Uses: Competition and general riding
Height: 16.1hh
Color: Any solid color

American Cream Draught Horse
Origins: The only draught breed to have originated in America
Description: A medium cream color with white mane and tail, pink skin and amber eyes. Strong and gentle
Height: 16.2hh
Color: Cream

Ardennais
Origins: France
Description: One of the world's leading heavy horses; powerful but very gentle
Height: 15hh to 16hh
Color: Varied but mainly roan, iron gray, chestnut, bay

Breton
Origins: France
Description: Compact bodies and short legs. Energetic and willing
Height: 15hh to 16.1hh
Color: Chestnut, gray or roan

Clydesdale
Origins: Scotland
Description: Long pasterns, a long arched neck and leg feathers (long hair in the fetlock area). They have a lively and free action
Height: 16-17hh
Color: Usually bay or brown with white on the face and legs

Freiberger
Origins: Switzerland
Description: Active mover, calm, good-natured, and sure-footed
Height: 15hh
Color: Bay or chestnut

Friesian
Origins: Holland
Description: A well-balanced horse with a noble look and kind temperament
Height: 15hh to 16hh
Color: Black

Italian Heavy Draught
Origins: Italy
Description: Attractive horse, stocky in build, can move at a good speed
Height: 15hh
Color: Mainly chestnut with flaxen mane and tail

Noriker
Origins: Austria
Description: Strong, tough with a calm temperament, sure-footed
Height: 16hh to 17hh
Color: Mainly brown

Guide to Draught Horses

Percheron
Origins: France. Arab influence, now one of the world's most popular work horses
Description: An attractive, well-proportioned horse with stamina
Height: 16.1hh
Color: Gray or black

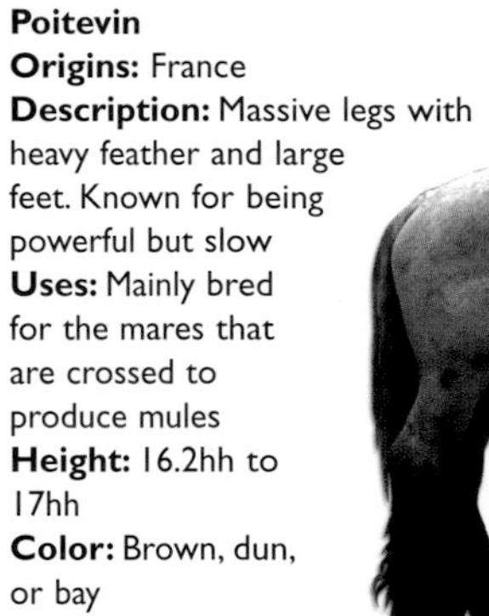

Poitevin
Origins: France
Description: Massive legs with heavy feather and large feet. Known for being powerful but slow
Uses: Mainly bred for the mares that are crossed to produce mules
Height: 16.2hh to 17hh
Color: Brown, dun, or bay

Shire
Origins: Britain
Description: Gentle giants of the horse world. Wide-chested with white markings and heavy feathers
Height: 16.2hh to 17.3hh
Color: Black, brown, gray, or bay

Suffolk Punch
Origins: Britain's oldest heavy breed
Description: They have a massive neck, square body and no feathers. Economical feeders and long-lived
Height: 16hh to 16.3hh
Color: Always "chesnut"

Basotho
Origins: Lesotho, South Africa
Description: Great stamina, quiet nature, endurance and sure-footedness. In addition to walk, trot, and canter, the Basotho has two extra gaits, the tripple and pace
Uses: Riding
Height: 14hh to 14.3hh
Color: Chestnut, gray, bay, brown, black

Caspian Pony
Origins: Iran
Description: Kind and tough, with great speed and endurance
Uses: Riding, jumping
Height: 10hh to 12hh
Color: Bay, gray, chestnut

Chincoteague Pony
Origins: United States
Description: Known for their striking looks, good nature, and intelligence
Height: 12hh to 13hh
Color: Any

Connemara
Origins: Connemara region of Ireland
Description: Compact, short-legged pony, brave but sensible
Uses: General riding, jumping, dressage, and driving
Height: 13hh to 14.2hh
Color: Gray but can also be brown, bay or black

Guide to Ponies

Dales
Origins: Pennine Hills, England
Description: Known for its strength and quiet nature. It has fine hair on the heels and powerful hindquarters
Uses: All-around riding and driving
Height: Up to 14.2hh
Color: Mainly black, bay, or brown

Dartmoor
Origins: Dartmoor, Devon
Description: A long-lived pony with a small head
Uses: Riding, driving, good child's pony
Height: Up to 12.2hh
Color: Usually black or brown

Eriskay
Origins: Rare breed originally native to the Western Isles of Scotland
Description: Strong with a thick, waterproof coat.
Uses: Riding and driving
Height: 12hh to 13.2hh
Color: Usually born black or bay, turning gray with maturity

Exmoor
Origins: Oldest of Britain's Mountain and Moorland breeds
Description: Very strong ponies, able to carry an adult
Uses: Riding and driving
Height: 12.2hh (mares), 13.2hh (stallions)
Color: Bay, brown, or dun with black points and light colored muzzle

Falabella
Origins: Argentina
Description: Perfectly proportioned miniature horse, resembling the Thoroughbred or Arab, although they are rarely bigger than 8hh
Uses: Showing, carting
Height: Under 8.2hh
Color: Any

Fjord
Origins: Norway
Description: Upright mane, strong, tough with short legs, sure-footed
Uses: Riding, driving
Height: 13hh to 14hh
Color: Dun in color with a stripe along the back

Gotland
Origins: Sweden
Description: Light and elegant pony, intelligent and gentle
Uses: Driving, children's ponies; they also make excellent trotters and jumpers
Height: 11.2hh to 13.hh
Color: Often dun or bay

Haflinger
Origins: Austria
Description: Sure-footed and tough, good tempered
Uses: Riding, driving, agriculture
Height: 14hh
Color: Chestnut with flaxen tail and mane

Highland
Origins: Scottish Highlands
Description: Strong and willing with striking coloring
Uses: Trekking, general riding driving, and competing
Height: 13hh to 14.2hh
Color: Dun, black or brown, bay, liver, chestnut with silver mane and tail

Hokkaido
Origins: Japan
Description: Hardy and strong
Uses: Trail riding, harness work
Height: 12.2hh to 13hh
Color: Most solid colors

Misaki
Origins: Japan
Description: Tough breed with relatively large head, thick and flowing mane
Uses: The breed has been designated a National Natural Treasure, and the herd has become the focus of tourism
Height: 12.2hh to 13.2hh
Color: Bay, black, chestnut

Pony of the Americas
Origins: United States
Description: Well proportioned, stylish, and refined
Uses: Good child's riding pony
Height: 11.2hh to 13.2hh
Color: Appaloosa markings

Pottok Pony
Origins: Southwest France
Description: Hardy and able to survive the most extreme conditions
Uses: Riding, competition
Height: 11hh to 14.2hh
Color: Black, bay, brown bay, chestnut, skewbald, or piebald

Shetland
Origins: Islands north east of Scotland
Description: Tough breed with an independent and headstrong nature; needs firm handling
Uses: Riding, driving
Height: 10.2hh
Color: Any, except spotted

Skyros Pony
Origins: Greece; now rare
Description: Small neat head, narrow body, straight shoulders, small feet
Uses: Riding
Height: 9.1hh to 1hh
Color: Dun, bay, gray

Welsh Pony
Origins: Wales
Four distinct breeds:
Section A: Maximum 12hh
Section B: Maximum 13.2hh, excellent riding pony
Section C: Cob type, maximum 13.2hh; good for driving
Section D: Average height 14.2hh; active and strong; useful for riding and driving
Color: Any solid color

Glossary

Aids
The methods used to communicate with a horse. Natural aids: legs, seat, and hands. Artificial aids: whip or spurs. Artificial aids are used as backup for the natural aids.

Bedding
The material placed on the floor of a stable to make it warm and comfortable for a horse. The most popular types are straw, wood shavings, and shredded paper.

Compound foods
Made of a variety of ingredients and are packaged to provide a balanced feed.

Concentrates
Energy-giving foods, such as barley and oats.

Conformation
The horse's overall form or shape.

Eohippus
An animal that lived more than 50 million years ago and from which the modern horse evolved.

Equus Caballus
Scientific name for the modern horse.

Equus
Name of the family of animals to which horses belong. It also includes zebras, mules, and donkeys.

Farrier
The name for the highly skilled person who cares for a horse's feet and fits iron shoes to the hooves.

Gaits
Ways of moving. A horse has four natural gaits – walk, trot, canter, and gallop.

Grooming
Keeping the horse healthy and clean by brushing the horse's coat, mane, and tail, as well as sponging the eyes, nostrils, and dock area.

Hand
A horse's height is measured in hands, from the ground to the withers. A hand is four inches. The letters 'hh' stand for hands high. Therefore, a horse said to be 15hh is 15 hands high.

Lame
Horses are said to be lame when an injury or illness, particularly to the foot or leg, affects the way of moving. Lame horses should not be ridden.

Mucking out
Keeping the horse's stable free of soiled bedding and dropping. This should be done on a daily basis for stabled horses.

Roughage
Bulky food, such as hay. It forms the main part of a horse's diet.

Tack
The equipment needed for riding a horse, the main pieces of which are the saddle and bridle.

Tacking up
The process of putting on the horse's tack, ready to be ridden.

Turnout
This can mean the way a horse is groomed and presented to be ridden, competed, or showed. It can also refer to the routine of turning a stabled horse out to grass during the day.

Untacking
The process of taking off the horse's tack.

Acknowledgements

Key: Top - t; middle - m; bottom - b; left - l; right - r;

Cover: Digital Stock **2-3:** Corel **4:** Corel. **5:** (t)Photos.com; (b)Corel. **8-10:** TT. **12:** Photos.com. **13:** Jim Channell. **14:** (t)Animal Photography; (b)Corel. **15:** Corel. **16:** Animal Photography. **17:** (t)Animal Photography; (b)Photos.com. **18-19:** Diana Morice. **20-21:** Kit Houghton. **22:** Animal Photography. **23:** (t)Photos.com; (b)Animal Photography. **24:** (t)Diana Morice; (b)Corbis. **25:** William Gottlieb/Corbis. **26:** Kit Houghton. **27:** Kit Houghton. **28:** (t)Kit Houghton. **28+29:** Alamy Images. **30:** Alamy images. **31:** Photos.com. **32:47:** Bob Langrish.